# EASTERN COUNTIES
## A NATIONAL BUS COMPANY

PETER HORREX AND TIM MOORE

AMBERLEY

First published 2018

Amberley Publishing
The Hill, Stroud
Gloucestershire, GL5 4EP

www.amberley-books.com



ISBN 978 1 4456 7961 7 (print)
ISBN 978 1 4456 7962 4 (ebook)



British Library Cataloguing in Publication Data.
A catalogue record for this book is available from the British Library.

Origination by Amberley Publishing.
Printed in the UK.

# Introduction

Registered on 14 July 1931, the Eastern Counties Omnibus Company Ltd was formed of four smaller operators across East Anglia and operated routes in Cambridgeshire, Norfolk and Suffolk, with some services reaching Lincolnshire and north Essex. Also at this time, the United coachworks was transferred to the new company, becoming Eastern Counties Coachworks in 1936. This facility became Eastern Coach Works (ECW), which would supply many buses to nationalised operators over the following decades. Part of the new Tilling Group from 1942, Eastern Counties became part of the National Bus Company on 1 July 1969, and it is this era that we focus on in this book.

## Livery

The new bus livery of poppy red and white was introduced in 1972, with the coaching stock becoming all-over white, both liveries incorporating the new double-N NBC logo. For a couple of years the fleet was in transition with some hybrid styles and differing shades of red on some vehicles, but the standard National corporate identity was soon strictly enforced by NBC headquarters in New Street Square, London. During the period of NBC ownership, the application of the livery evolved to include a red and blue double-N on a white square for buses from 1976, and there was a period where no white band was applied to saloons.

## Vehicles

The NBC years saw the demise of some stalwarts, such as Bristol MW medium-weight saloons and Bristol Lodekka double-deckers. In fact Eastern Counties was one of the last NBC companies to use the Bristol Lodekka in significant numbers, with crew operation finally ending at the close of 1983 in Norwich.

New vehicle policy was quite standardised during the NBC years, with the Bristol VRT with Eastern Coach Works bodywork becoming the standard double-decker. Single-deck orders started with the Bristol RE and Bristol LH, also with ECW bodywork, with later orders concentrating on the Leyland National integral. Coaches and dual-purpose vehicles were initially Bristol RELH, and later largely Leyland Leopards with bodywork by Plaxton, Duple, Alexander and Willowbrook. Leyland Tigers and double-deck MCW Metroliners made an appearance in later years. A sprinkling of variety was provided by oddities such as the Ford Transit community buses and the solitary Ford A Series, which didn't last long. In the last couple of years the minibus revolution was in full swing with large numbers of Transits, Sherpas and Mercedes types across the fleet.

## Deregulation

In preparation for deregulation the following year, Eastern Counties was split into three in September 1984, with most of the old Western Area (Cambridge and Peterborough) operations passing to a newly formed company called Cambus Ltd. The coaching operations passed to another new company, Ambassador Travel (Eastern Counties) Ltd, the fleetname Ambassador Travel having been used by Eastern Counties for some of its coaching operations in the previous few months. The remainder of the old Eastern Counties continued as the operating company for bus services in what was the old Eastern Area, and passed into private ownership in 1987 following a management buy-out.

VR390 (BNG 452J) turns around at Levington in Suffolk on 10 April 1982. Levington is a small village just outside Ipswich and is probably best known for Fisons Levington compost, Fisons having a research station on the edge of the village. This afternoon journey on route 250 was often linked with a mid-afternoon journey on route 851 from Ipswich to Norwich and back. (Photograph: Peter Horrex)

LWC 982J was a Bristol RELH6G with forty-seven seats in her Plaxton Panorama Elite body, new to Eastern National in 1971. She was transferred to National Travel (South East) in 1974, and to Eastern Counties in 1978, where she was numbered RE847, and is pictured on the parking area near Hills Road depot in Cambridge on 2 November 1981. On the nearside RE847 has the logo for 'Eastern Counties 50 years of service 1931 – 1981' and branding for the London–Cambridge Motorway Service that used the M11 motorway. (Photograph: Robert Appleton)

In 1973 an agreement was made between NBC and SBG (Scottish Bus Group) to exchange FLF/VRT vehicles on a one-for-one basis. The FLFs had to be 1967 or newer and Eastern Counties sent forty-six 1967/8 FLFs. However, sixteen of the VRTs were diverted to Eastern National and Lincolnshire with older FLFs from these fleets joining ECOC. In this picture, FLF435 (BVL 45C), dating from 1965 and transferred from Lincolnshire, loads in Norwich bus station for the 23-mile journey to Cromer on the north Norfolk coast. This bus has the Cave-Brown-Cave heating system, which was not a common feature in the Eastern Counties fleet. (Photograph: Tim Moore)

Eastern Counties RL679 (RAH 679F) met an early end when she was destroyed by fire a few months after this photograph was taken, while working in service between Aldeburgh and Ipswich. In this 1980 view she is seen at Mistley, Rigby Avenue, having turned around ready for her return journey to Ipswich. (Photograph: Peter Horrex)

Seen here on the now pedestrianised Gentleman's Walk in Norwich, FLF428 (LCW 666C) negotiates its way past a Ford Escort van en route to Hellesdon, a northern suburb. The bus is a 1965 Bristol FLF6G with seventy-seat ECW bodywork and was transferred from Eastern National in 1973 as part of the FLF/VRT bus swap between the National Bus Company and Scottish Bus Group. (Photograph: Tim Moore)

LL748–54 (MCL 930–6P) were Leopard type PSU3C/4R and the Alexander T type bodies seated forty-nine passengers. Dual-purpose white/red livery was carried when new in April 1976 but the whole batch were repainted into white coach livery by 1978. After a short time in service, problems with cooling led to an additional grille being fitted between the fog lights and above the registration number, as can be seen in this view taken on Castle Meadow in Norwich on 28 May 1977. (Photograph: Peter Horrex collection)

In the late 1970s the Ipswich to Stradbroke service via Woodbridge and Framlingham was renumbered from 203 to 273, and subsequently a variation of 274 was also introduced, with the 274 operating via Laxfield, and the 273 via Brundish and Wilby. In the hands of the Woodbridge outstation, Eastern Counties RLE869 (WPW 869H) poses for the camera at Brundish in 1983. (Photograph: Peter Horrex)

RL734 (YVF 734J) with an East Bergholt outstation crew at Rigby Avenue, Mistley, in August 1974. At this time service 209 operated from Ipswich to Mistley via Tattingstone, Brantham, East End, East Bergholt, Cattawade and Manningtee. RL734 was a Bristol RELL6G with an Eastern Coach Works fifty-three-seat body and was new in 1970. (Photograph: Robert Appleton)

An unusual view of LFS112 (FAH 112C) taken from Norwich Castle mound on 24 March 1980. The bus, a Bristol FS5G with sixty-seat Eastern Coach Works bodywork, was delivered in July 1965, one of twenty-six that year. (Photograph: Tim Moore)

A line-up of Bristol FS5G Lodekkas in the old railway yard at Cambridge on 26 June 1977. All except one of the buses shown carry the facelifted style of grille and cream window rubbers introduced in 1962, and the six buses nearest the camera can be identified as LFS107 (DNG 107C), LFS54 (54CPW), LFS95 (CVF 295B), LFS70 (70 DPW), LFS45 (45 CNG) and LFS55 (55 CPW). (Photograph: Tim Moore)

VR270 (RAH 270W) at Ipswich when brand new in 1981. Allocated to the Saxmundham depot, she is waiting to depart from Ipswich on the 16.40 273 service to Stradbroke on a Saturday evening. (Photograph: Peter Horrex)

Seen in Norwich bus station is Bristol RELL6G RL718 on 22 July 1980. The bus was one of seven Bristol RELL6Gs delivered to Eastern Counties with forty-eight-seat dual-door bodywork in 1969/70, RL718 being the last to arrive from ECW in April 1970. All seven were converted to standard single-door layout in 1972, becoming B52F. RL718 had additional grilles on the offside beneath the windows and opening roof vents due to the vehicle being fitted with an experimental heating system from new. (Photograph: Tim Moore)

VR396 (ENG 396K) is working from Ipswich to Stradbroke in this 1980 view, and she is pictured here turning around at Laxfield. This was achieved by either reversing onto the open area behind her, or pulling past the triangle at the road junction and reversing back. VR396 was delivered new in Tilling red and cream livery in March 1972, and, along with VRs 397/8 were the last VRs delivered in this livery. (Photograph: Peter Horrex)

In 1979–80 there was a large influx of thirty coaches into the Eastern Counties fleet, comprising Leyland Leopards with Plaxton, Duple and Willowbrook bodywork (LL792–813 and LP814–21). A Leyland Leopard PSU3E/4R with Plaxton C49F bodywork, LP819 (JVF 819V) is seen here in the picturesque village of Kersey in Suffolk in the long hot summer of 1983. (Photograph: Tim Moore)

New in February 1978, VR207 (XNG 207S) was allocated to the Ipswich depot, and, as was standard practice at the time, the newest VR was used on the 204 service to Bury St Edmunds. She is seen here when two years old in 1980 on a Saturday evening while working the 1830 service from Ipswich, collecting passengers at Stowmarket. (Photograph: Peter Horrex)

LH697 (VAH 697H) was a Bristol LH6P with an Eastern Coach Works forty-five seat body new in 1969, and is seen at Rigby Avenue, Mistley, in May 1977. Service 221 operated from Ipswich to Mistley via Holbrook, Stutton, Brantham, Cattawade and Manningtree. (Photograph: Robert Appleton)

In this view at Great Yarmouth depot taken on 10 August 1980, we see from left: LL837 (HRN 956G), a Plaxton-bodied Leyland Leopard PSU3A/4R new in 1969 but acquired from Ribble the previous year; RE850 (SAH 850M), a Bristol RELH6G/Plaxton new in 1974; RE897 (SVF 897G), a Bristol RELH6G/ECW new in 1969; RE846 (LWC 981J), another Bristol RELH6G/Plaxton, new to Eastern National in 1971, but which was acquired from National Travel (South East) in 1978; LL838 (RVF 838R), a Leyland Leopard PSU3D/4R with Plaxton bodywork new as LC838 in 1976; and at the far end an unidentified Bristol RELH6G/ECW. (Photograph: Tim Moore)

VR302 (LFS 304F) was one of the VRs that came to Eastern Counties in 1973 as part of the exchange of Lodekkas for VRs between the National Bus Company and the Scottish Bus Group. She is seen here in 1980 at Felixstowe while crew-operated, having arrived on service 252 from Ipswich. (Photograph: Peter Horrex)

The winter of 1983/84 had some quite unpleasant days and this view shows VR147 (GNG 713N), a 1975 VRT/SL6G with Eastern Coach Works standard seventy-four-seat bodywork, in Norwich bus station, having arrived from East Dereham on service 834 in the morning peak. (Photograph: Tim Moore)

Leyland National (type 1151/1R/0501) LN547 (HVF 547L) had been new in 1973. From a driver's point of view they were a different beast to what had come before and early models could be quite unforgiving in certain conditions, such as wet or icy roads. No such problems here in the lovely summer of 1984, as LN547 passes the top of Timberhill in Norwich on its way to Drayton (Cator Road). (Photograph: Tim Moore)

The Woodbridge outstation had this lovely Wednesday only journey to Harleston in Norfolk. The journey was linked to a morning school journey to Framlingham, then a service journey via Strabroke to Pulham Market and Pulham St Mary, ending in Harleston where the driver had something like a two-hour break, allowing the passengers time to complete their shopping, before the return journey was worked. Here we see Eastern Counties LH930 (WEX 930S) collecting passengers at Pulham St Mary in 1985. (Photograph: Peter Horrex)

From 1980, Leyland Nationals were delivered to the new updated design known as the 'National 2', which featured, among the most obvious visual changes, a more bulbous front incorporating a front-mounted radiator. LN610 (PEX 610W) was one of nineteen National 2s delivered in 1980 (LN601–19) and is seen here at Cringleford (School) terminus in July 1984. (Photograph: Tim Moore)

The Old Cattle Market bus station in Ipswich had adjacent to it a depot building along with offices and the staff canteen, with the main depot and engineering facilities being a five-minute walk away in the Foundation Street and Star Lane area of the town. In this 1979 view we see Eastern Counties LM630 (FPW 630C) and LHS932 (WNG 101H) in between journeys in the depot area adjacent to the bus station. (Photograph: Peter Horrex)

LS809 (3809 PW) was a Bristol MW6G with thirty-nine coach seats in her Eastern Coach Works body, new in 1962. In March 1976 she was converted to one-man operation, but retained the coach seats. Pictured departing from Ipswich Old Cattle Market bus station on service 208 to Harkstead in July 1976. (Photograph: Robert Appleton)

As previously mentioned, Ipswich depot always tried to allocate their newest type Bristol VR to the jointly operated 204 service to Bury St Edmunds. With the arrival of four new VRs at the end of 1979, this honour fell to VR243 (JAH 243V), relieving VR207, which had previously been used. In this January 1980 view 243 is seen collecting passengers at Woolpit on what would have been the 10.30 departure from Ipswich on a Saturday morning. (Photograph: Peter Horrex)

Eastern Counties standardised on the Bristol FLF6G chassis with seventy-seat Eastern Coach Works (ECW) bodywork for the last three years of half-cab orders, following which the Bristol VR became the standard double decker. Between 1966 and 1968, a total of eighty-two new FLFs entered the fleet, FLF441 (GPW 441D) lays over at the Hellesdon (Parkway) terminus in Norwich in November 1981. (Photograph: Tim Moore)

In the care of the Woodbridge outstation is LN782 (DPW 782T), displaying the large bold fleetname on her front panels, which started to appear in 1985. She is seen here at Dennington, awaiting departure time back to Woodbridge on service 273. (Photograph: Peter Horrex)

One of the more low profile and least successful Eastline routes was the 791 between Bury St Edmunds and Norwich. On 20 August 1982, RE851 (SAH 851M) is seen in the old Bury St Edmunds bus station in Brentgovel Street, preparing to load for Norwich. RE851 was one of four Bristol RELH6G coaches with Plaxton forty-nine-seat bodies and power doors delivered in 1974 in National white coach livery, and passed to Cambus in September 1984. (Photograph: Tim Moore)

New in 1977, LC839 (SPW 105R) was the second Plaxton-bodied Leyland Leopard to be delivered and the registration followed on from Duple Dominant LL755–8 (SPW 101–4R). The first was LC838 (RVF 838R), delivered in 1976. LC839 is seen here outside Central Works in Cremorne Lane, Norwich, soon after delivery from Plaxtons on 25 April 1977. Note the body builder's sticker in the side window. (Photograph: Tim Moore)

New in 1980, VR247 (KVF 247V) was a Bristol VRT/SL3/6LXB with Eastern Coach Works seventy-four-seat body. On 13 April 1982, VR247 was on layover on the coach and bus park off Westgate in Peterborough. Speedline was the branding applied to bus services in Peterborough connecting the city centre with the new Orton townships. However, VR247 displayed route number X51, which was the limited-stop version of service 151, Peterborough–Cambridge. (Photograph: Robert Appleton)

The full length of the Bristol RELL can be seen in this 1980 view in the Old Cattle Market bus station in Ipswich of RL513 (EPW 513K), which was delivered new in March 1972. (Photograph: Peter Horrex)

East Bergholt outstation was closed in January 1981 with its buses moving to Cattawade. In June 1983 Cattawade outstation was closed, and the buses moved back to East Bergholt. The garage building had been sold, so the buses parked on the forecourt. There, on 2 December 1984, were Bristol VRT series 3 VR243 (JAH 243V) and VR189 (RPW 189R), with Bristol VRT series 2 VR405 (KPW 405L) in the middle. (Photograph: Robert Appleton)

Bristol VR, VR258 (RAH 258W) stands alongside two Bristol RE buses, RL507 (CNG 507K) and RL680 (RAH 680F), at Ipswich in 1980. Closest to the camera, RL680 shows the earlier flat-screen style bodywork, with RL507 displaying the later curved screen style. (Photograph: Peter Horrex)

FLF457 (JPW 457D) was a Bristol FLF6G/ECW Lodekka new in 1966. Seen here on St Stephen's roundabout in Norwich on 22 July 1980, it is operating service 521 to Eaton Park , the small yellow 'V' under the fleet number denoting it is based at Vulcan Road depot, the smaller of the two Norwich depots at that time. (Photograph: Tim Moore)

*Above, below and opposite above*: In 1980, an unmanned compound off Barker Street in Norwich was used for the storage of surplus and withdrawn vehicles. On 28 May 1980 there was an arson attack that left several vehicles destroyed, including withdrawn Bristol FS5G/ECW LFS115 (FAH 115C), which was left completely gutted. It was sold to local scrap dealer J. Bagshaw two months later, together with the remains of sister LFS118 (FAH 118C), Bristol LH6P/ECW (RAH 692F) and Bristol RELH/ECW RE887 (GVF 887D), which were also severely damaged. (Photograph: Tim Moore)

FLF440 (GPW 440D) was one of the last four Lodekkas to work from Ispwich depot, while RLE869 (WPW 869H) was to be the last RE, being transferred to Norwich in April 1985, though Bristol REs did return to Ipswich for two very brief spells later on. FLF440, which had been new in 1966, was withdrawn in 1982, whereas RLE869 still survives today in preservation. This photograph was taken in Ipswich in 1979. (Photograph: Peter Horrex)

An unusual purchase in 1984 were LT900–2 (A900–2 KAH), high-floor fifty-seat Plaxton Paramount 3500-bodied Leyland Tiger TRCTL11/3RH in Ambassador Holidays livery. At this time Ambassador had not been separated from Eastern Counties, as evidenced by the EC fleetname on the first side window and the ECOC legal lettering. All three of these coaches passed to Ambassador Travel (Eastern Counties) Ltd when EC split in September 1984. (Photograph: Tim Moore)

VR401 (OCK 101K) was a Bristol VRT/SL6G series 2 with Eastern Coach Works seventy-seat body new to Ribble in 1972, and acquired by Eastern Counties in 1985. On 7 October 1986, VR401 was at Sudbury Upper School working from Sudbury outstation on service 193 from Sudbury to Acton, a Suffolk County Council tendered service. (Photograph: Robert Appleton)

Seen here on 12 August 1980 at the Lodge Lane, Old Catton, terminus in Norwich is FLF448 (HPW 448D), a Bristol FLF6G with standard ECW seventy-seat bodywork. It has been freshly repainted for probably the last time, as the type disappeared from normal service at the end of 1983. (Photograph: Tim Moore)

In 1969, Eastern Counties took into stock early examples of the Bristol VRT/SL with Eastern Coach Works seventy-seat bodywork, its first double-deckers with semi-automatic transmission. VR379 is seen here in May 1978 in Norwich preparing to depart for Bungay on service 871 via Poringland and Brooke. The bus was withdrawn in early 1985, passing initially to Ben Jordan, Coltishall, in July 1985 and then to Ripley, Carlton, for scrap in September the same year. (Photograph: Tim Moore)

In 1985 Eastern Counties purchased four Alexander-bodied Leyland Leopards from West Riding, one of which, LL788 (PWW 706R), is photographed here leaving Ipswich for Sudbury in 1986. (Photograph: Peter Horrex)

LN770 (XNG 770S) was a Phase 2 Leyland National of type 11351A/1R delivered in July 1978. The Phase 2 model was introduced in 1976 in response to operational experience and incorporated a number of improvements to improve comfort and handling. LN770 is captured in Brigg Street, Norwich, in August 1984 having come along Gentleman's Walk, which is now pedestrianised. (Photograph: Tim Moore)

This view of LH915 (YPW 915J), a Bristol LH6P with a Perkins engine and Eastern Coach Works forty-five-seat bus body, was recorded in March 1973 at a time when many variants of NBC livery were being applied, including a darker red and non-standard application of relief colours. LH915 has been repainted, it would seem, in poppy red and white, but with the white applied to the window surrounds in the same style as the cream of the previous Tilling livery. This was not the only LH so treated, but the standard livery of a white band below the windows was soon introduced. (Photograph: Tim Moore)

To keep light running costs to a minimum, Eastern Counties historically had a large number of outstations in rural areas. Of course, historically buses would have been of smaller dimensions (probably around 9 metres) and the outstation doors could be closed at night, but by the time this view of Mundesley outstation was recorded in July 1978 the allocation was of long saloons, in this case 11.3-metre Leyland Nationals. Outstations were gradually abandoned as rural services declined, and in common with many locations Mundesley was closed on 27 November 1982 and the site later sold for housing. (Photograph: Tim Moore)

A boost to the single-deck fleet was the surprise acquisition of nine Bristol RELL6Gs with ECW bodies in 1981. These differed from other RLs in the fleet by having only forty-nine seats plus a luggage pen in lieu of a front bench seat. They were numbered RL685–93, and seen here arriving at Great Yarmouth bus station via the back entrance in 1983 is RL691 (CMO 647J), which was new in May 1971. The bus was sold for scrap in July 1984. (Photograph: Tim Moore)

In September 1986 Eastern Counties gained the Suffolk County Council contract for Saturdays-only service 194 from Sudbury to Colchester via Assington, Polstead, and Langham, with one journey in each direction. On 27 December 1986, VR135 (SNG 135M), outstationed at Sudbury, was collecting passengers at Colchester bus station for the return journey to Sudbury. VR135 was a Bristol VRT/SL6G series 2 with an Eastern Coach Works seventy-four-seat body, new in 1974. (Photograph: Robert Appleton)

For many years the Norwich recovery truck was X38, a 1947-built AEC Matador with a 1961 body, which had replaced the original military-style bodywork. Seen here outside Central Works on 12 April 1976 recovering accident-damaged VR137 (SNG 437M), it was withdrawn in 1978, being replaced by Ford D series X61 (JGU 562K). (Photograph: Tim Moore)

In the first half of 1985, four high-bridge (14 foot 6 inch) Series 2 VRTs were acquired from Hastings & District that had been new to Maidstone & District in 1975 as 5731–4 (KKE 731–4N). Numbered HVR331–4 in the Eastern Counties fleet and all allocated to Norwich city services, they initially entered service in NBC green but soon received repaints into poppy red but with yellow central bands and roofs to distinguish them as higher vehicles. Here we see HVR333 (KKE 733N) pressed into service in NBC green but with EC fleetnames in May 1985. (Photograph: Tim Moore)

Norwich, Surrey Street, in August 1984 and we have a good comparison of the three Leyland National frontal styles to be seen at that time in Norwich. Furthest from the camera is standard Leyland National 2 LN604 (KVG 604V), in the middle is National 1 LN767 (XNG 767S), and closest to the photographer is the Gardner engine conversion LG781 (DPW 781T), which would receive a standard National 2 front the following year. (Photograph: Tim Moore)

A nationwide advertising campaign took place in 1981/2 for National Holidays, the programme of tours operated on behalf of National Bus by their local bus and coach subsidiaries. The vehicles chosen by Eastern Counties for this livery were quite special in themselves, being delivered in NBC green from United Counties. VR297 was allocated to Norwich, where it is seen a month later in November 1981 on service 554 to Lakenham. (Photograph: Tim Moore)

*Above and below*: VR205 (XNG 205S), a standard Bristol VRT/SL3 with a seventy-four-seat Eastern Coach Works body, was selected in May 1978 to promote Eastern Counties Anywhere Tickets, which had replaced the original Wanderbus Tickets following the adoption of the Wanderbus name by National Bus for their own inter-company rover tickets. Prices of tickets were shown on the waistband, which were regularly changed as prices rose. VR205 later received other advertising liveries including Radio Broadland and Norwich Energy Action. (Photograph: Tim Moore)

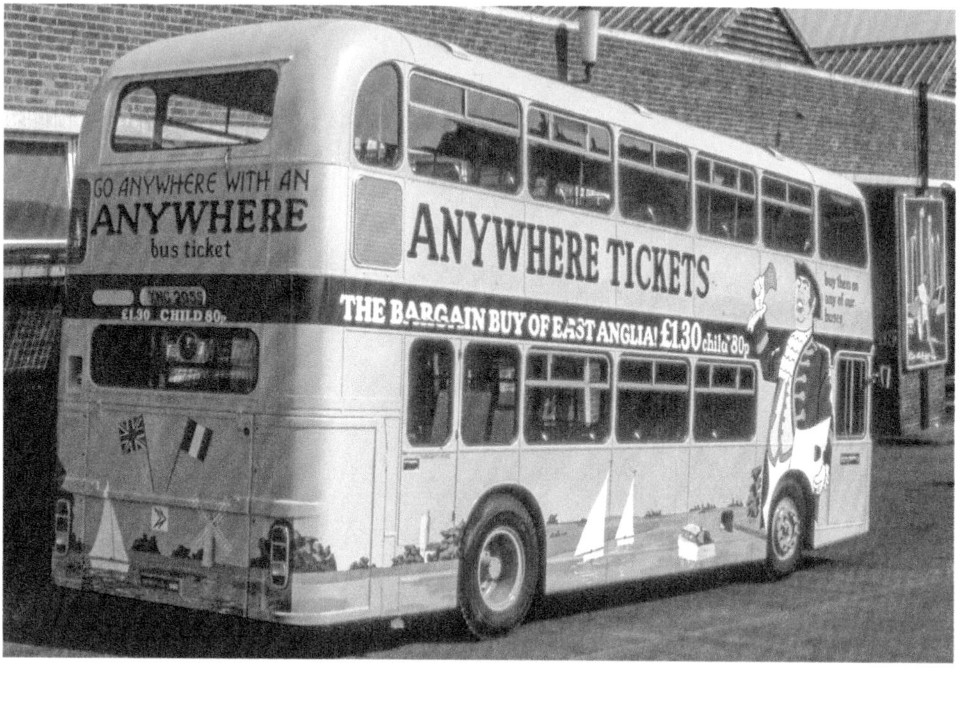

A picturesque scene here from 1980 as Leyland National LN598 (WVF 598S) heads out of Shottisham in Suffolk. Delivered new with seating for fifty-two, she had this downgraded to forty-nine seats in March 1980 when a luggage pen was fitted. (Photograph: Peter Horrex)

New in 1970, RLE862 (WNG 862H) was a Bristol RELL6G with an Eastern Coach Works body with fifty dual-purpose seats. Allocated to Bury St Edmunds, in July 1976 RLE862 was leaving the Old Cattle Market bus station in Ipswich, working home on service 204 to Bury St Edmunds. (Photograph: Robert Appleton)

Two seventy-seat ECW-bodied Bristol LDL open-toppers (VDV752/3) were acquired from Devon General in May 1979 and numbered OT1 and OT2 in the EC fleet. OT1 was branded as 'Seaside Special' for use between Sheringham and Overstrand and is seen here on 28 May 1978 in Cromer bus station with a light load. (Photograph: Tim Moore)

Bristol RELL6G RL862 (WNG 862H) was delivered in February 1970 as dual-purpose RLE872. By the time this view was recorded in early 1984 the vehicle had been downgraded to bus status and renumbered RL862, though it retained fifty dual-purpose seats. (Photograph: Tim Moore)

*Above and left*: FLF456 (JPW 456D) is seen here in Castle Meadow in November 1983, waiting to depart for Costessey. The JPW batch (FLF 454–9) were fitted with a different staircase arrangement with shallower stairs, meaning that one extra was fitted, together with a more angular and shorter upper deck staircase surround with a single rail more like a VR. (Photograph: Tim Moore)

New in January 1971, Eastern Counties RL735 (AAH 735J) is pictured in Norwich in November 1977, wearing the overall advertising livery for sending your parcels by bus. RL735 was painted into this livery in September 1972, receiving a repaint into the same livery nine years later in the summer of 1981. She was finally painted into NBC poppy red in September 1984, passing to Cambus on the split of Eastern Counties that same month. (Photograph: Peter Horrex collection)

HVR334 (KKE 734N) is seen at Norwich bus station, posing for the camera following its transformation from Hastings & District NBC green into poppy red livery in June 1985. The bus was one of four acquired earlier in the year. The yellow relief colour was applied for the benefit of controllers and drivers so at a glance this batch of four buses could be identified as unsuitable for work other than on city routes due to their 14-foot 6-inch height. (Photograph: Tim Moore)

The trusty recovery vehicle for many years in Norwich was X38, a 1947 AEC Matador, which ran on trade plates 591 PW. Here on 21 June 1977 she is recovering accident-damaged RL520 (Bristol RELL6G/ECW), which had been involved in a fatal accident near Holt, in which the car driver sadly died. The bus received a major frontal rebuild at Central Works and gave many more years of service. (Photograph: Tim Moore)

RS647 (KVF 647E) was a Bristol RESL6G with an Eastern Coach Works forty-six seat body, new in 1967. On 17 July 1981, RS647 was found parked in the yard at Bury St Edmunds depot. (Photograph: Robert Appleton)

Seen here with its crew, the late Derek Lambert (conducting) and Mark Brighton, LFS91 (CNG 291B), a Bristol FS5G with Eastern Coach Works sixty-seat bodywork, waits in the summer sunshine on 12 June 1980 at Bowthorpe (Wendene). At this time the bus was in its sixteenth year of service, but it would be withdrawn the following year. (Photograph: Tim Moore)

In September 1984, VR251 (PCL 251W) received a Colourbus all-over advertisement for Radio Broadland, a fairly new local radio station at the time. The bus was fitted with an in-cab car radio, which fed speakers on both decks. Here VR251 is seen shortly after receiving the livery in Brigg Street, Norwich, en route for Hellesdon, a northern suburb. (Photograph: Tim Moore)

*Above and below*: Here we see the only Leyland National in the EC fleet to be converted to Gardner power. LN600 (WVF 600S) sadly suffered a fatal accident and was withdrawn when relatively new in December 1979. As the back end was undamaged, the decision was made to use the vehicle as a test bed for the installation of a Gardner 6HLX engine, as used in Bristol RE vehicles. The installation and testing were deemed successful and LN781 (DPW 781T) was selected as the operational vehicle to be converted to Gardner 6HLX power in June 1981, a project which included fitting a front mounted radiator and raising the rear floor level by about 2 inches to accommodate the larger engine. Renumbered LG781, the bus was involved in an accident with LN605 and suffered frontal damage in January 1985. As the front of LN605 was undamaged, and as the modular construction of Leyland Nationals permitted it, the front end of LN605 was fitted to LG781, thus changing the appearance to that of a National 2. LN605 was then scrapped. The original design is seen here in 1984 in Norwich bus station (*above*) while the Mark 2 front has been fitted in the view taken at the university in 1985 (*below*). (Photograph: Tim Moore)

VR185 (PEX 385R) was delivered new in August 1976 and was captured working Ipswich local service 218 at Claydon in 1980. Route 218 supplemented the main Ipswich to Stowmarket/Bury St Edmunds and Ipswich to Norwich services, which all passed through Claydon, though the 218 served through the housing estate before returning to Ipswich. (Photograph: Peter Horrex)

In the 1980s, Norwich Lodekkas were parked out in the bus station at night. Here we see the early part of the run in on 14 July 1979, with LFS121 (FVF 421C) parked up following a stint on city route 554 (Sprowston to Lakenham) with LFS106 on the right, which had run in from one of the 501 group services (all short workings to the bus station were numbered 503). Both were withdrawn in 1980 and went to Ben Jordan for scrap. (Photograph: Tim Moore)

Eastern Counties was notable for operating all three main height variants of the VRT/ECW. Seen here in August 1984 in Surrey Street depot in Norwich are examples of the three most common heights. From the left are: standard low-height 13-feet 8-inches VR288 (VEX 288X), new in 1981; high-bridge 14-feet 6-inches HVR334 (KKE 734N), new to Maidstone & District in 1975; and super-low-height 13-feet 5-inches VR411 (CJO 471R), new to City of Oxford in 1977. The differences in height are easily identified by the depth (or absence) of the central colour band. (Photograph: Tim Moore)

RL665 (PPW 665F), new in 1968, was numerically the first of the RL class of Bristol RELL6G with Eastern Coach Works fifty-three-seat bodies. On 22 July 1981, RL665 was in St Andrews Street North at Bury St Edmunds, working a town service. To the left of the fleetname is the logo for Eastern Counties' fiftieth anniversary, which read 'Eastern Counties 1931 – 1981 50 years of service'. (Photograph: Robert Appleton)

*Above and below*: Leyland National LN783 (DPW 783T) was new in February 1979. It was repainted in January 1980 as part of a nationwide recruitment campaign by the Army. In what was basically an upside-down version of the dual-purpose livery of the time, the lower half was painted white with green lettering, which was fine when it was clean but looked awful after a few minutes on country roads in bad weather! The livery lasted about a year until it reverted to fleet livery in April 1981. These views were recorded in Norwich depot at the end of February 1980, the bus later operating at various depots as part of the promotion. (Photographs: Peter Horrex collection)

VR189 (RPW 189R) was part of an order for Waveney District Council, but was taken by Eastern Counties when that council ceased to operate. She was photographed here at Dennington in Suffolk in 1985 while in the care of the Woodbridge outstation. (Photograph: Peter Horrex)

By 1977, fifty-six Leyland Nationals had been taken into stock, all with Leyland 510 engines and fifty-two-seat bodywork. Phase 2 model LN593 (WAH 593S) stands on Castle Meadow in Norwich on 29 June 1979. The turbocharged Leyland 510 engine was notoriously smoky, and staining from the fishtail exhaust can be seen on the lower panels at the rear. The exhausts on LNs were later modified to exit centrally from under the rear bumper. (Photograph: Tim Moore)

Following on from the Norfolk Flyer-liveried Leyland Tigers (LT887–94, EAH 887–94Y), a further two similar coaches with Plaxton Paramount 3200 fifty-seat bodies with toilets were delivered in December 1983, these being LT895/6 (A895/6KCL) in full National Express stripey livery. LT895 is seen emerging from Surrey Street depot in May 1984, a few months before being swapped with Midland Red (Express) along with LT890/6 for Metroliners ML903–5 (A666–8 XDA) in August. (Photograph: Tim Moore)

A Bristol VRT/SL3 with standard Eastern Coach Works seventy-four-seat bodywork, VR210 (YNG 210S) is pictured at Norwich Central Works shortly after delivery in June 1978, and was one of twenty-three similar vehicles taken into stock that year. (Photograph: Tim Moore)

The 1983 intake of new vehicles consisted entirely of Leyland Tigers with Plaxton Paramount 3200 bodywork. The first were LT887–94 (EAH 887–94Y) in March 1983, which were delivered in a distinctive blue and white Norfolk Flyer livery for the National Express 099 service between Norwich and London. Before use on express work they were used over Easter on gentler excursion work to run them in. LT891 is seen here on a day tour to the Pennines on 4 April 1983, stopping to offer passengers a photographic opportunity. (Photograph: Tim Moore)

Allocated to Bury St Edmunds and outstationed at Walsham-le-Willows, RL504 (BVF 667J) was at Diss bus park on 12 March 1982 having worked 1000 Garboldisham–Diss service 920, a Fridays-only service, with Friday being Diss' market day. RL504 was a Bristol RELL6G with an Eastern Coach Works fifty-three-seat body, new in 1981. (Photograph: Robert Appleton)

Following the purchase of the first Leyland Leopards in 1976, more of the type were taken in 1977 with both Plaxton and Duple bodywork. Seen outside Central Works in Norwich shortly after delivery in May 1977, LL758 (SPW104R) was the last of four PSU3E/4R Leopards with Duple Dominant forty-nine-seat bodies to bus grant specification, which included power doors to allow use on stage carriage work. (Photograph: Tim Moore)

New in November 1979, LL808 (JCL 808V) was a Leyland Leopard PSU3E/4R with a new style of body to the fleet, the Willowbrook 003, and was numerically the second coach to carry this bodywork. Eventually sixteen of the type would be acquired (LL792–800, LL807–13), LL808 is seen here on 15 March 1980 in Norwich bus station, awaiting departure to London. (Photograph: Tim Moore)

The first of Eastern Counties' flat-screened Bristol RE buses came in April 1968 in the form of RL665 (PPW 665F), pictured here at King's Lynn on 27 April 1985. When delivered she was not fitted out for driver-only operation, and ran crew-operated until the autumn of 1968. She was withdrawn in 1986. (Photograph: Peter Horrex collection)

VR198 (TEX 408R) is seen here outside Central Works in Norwich following delivery from Eastern Coach Works at Lowestoft in May 1977. The Pay As You Enter (PAYE) illuminating sign has yet to be fitted on the front dash, these being added after delivery by Central Works staff. VR198 was one of thirteen Bristol VRT/SL3s received in 1977, and remained with Eastern Counties after the Cambus company was formed in 1984. (Photograph: Tim Moore)

New in 1974, RLE743 (GCL 345N) was a Bristol RELH6L with an Eastern Coach Works body fitted with forty-nine dual-purpose seats. In 1981 her Leyland 0.680 engine was replaced by a Gardner 6HLX unit. In 1984 she was repainted into bus livery and reclassified RL743, but retained the dual-purpose seats. RL743 was pictured in Queensgate bus station in Peterborough on 21 June 1984, working from Oundle outstation. (Photograph: Robert Appleton)

Sitting in the early evening sunshine at Norwich, Vulcan Road, depot on 29 May 1980 are Leyland Nationals LN604 (KVG 604V) and LN767 (XNG 767S). Clearly showing the difference in frontal styling between the Mark 1 (LN767) and Mark 2 (LN604) models, the buses have just run in for the night and have been fuelled and washed. LN604 had been new in February that year while LN767 dates from July 1978. (Photograph: Tim Moore)

Delivered in March 1966, FLF446 was the seventh new FLF that year. When new, fixed glass was fitted to the upper deck on both sides, though the push out vents at the front were retained. Ventilation was provided by five ball vents each side of the roof. Normal hopper windows were eventually fitted years later but only then in alternate bays. FLF446 is seen here in Norwich bus station on 14 May 1978 and clearly shows the original arrangement. (Photograph: Tim Moore)

VR281 (VAH 281X) was a Bristol VRT/SL3/6LXB with an Eastern Coach Works seventy-four seat body, new in 1981. Allocated to Bury St Edmunds, she was standing outside her home depot on 21 June 1984 when seen. (Photograph: Robert Appleton)

Seen at Peterborough, Lincoln Road, depot on 12 September 1975 is Ford Transit 175 pickup truck X60 (HEX 703N). The X series was reserved for service vehicles, while the Y series was for staff cars, but details of these have never been published. (Photograph: Tim Moore)

VRT/SL3 deliveries commenced at VR161 in 1976. Illustrated here at Buckingham Road terminus in Norwich on a snowy day in December 1981, VR171 (MEX 768P) had been new in February 1976. Together with VR170, from new it was fitted with Sevcon automatic transmission, which proved unsatisfactory, and both received normal semi-automatic transmission in November 1976. (Photograph: Tim Moore)

*Left and below*: In January 1978, Bristol FS5G training bus X65 (ex-LFS124, GNG 124C) was hit in the rear end by an HGV while on training duties near Newmarket. The lorry completely demolished the staircase and the bus was deemed uneconomic to repair. A replacement bus was acquired from Eastern National in the form of their early model FLF6G 2717 (97 TVX), which was delivered to Cremorne Lane Central Works in NBC green. It is seen here on 4 May 1978, repainted into the yellow training bus livery and numbered X67 in the Eastern Counties fleet, following on from X66, a training FS. To enable the instructor to sit behind the driver, the staircase on X67 was removed and an additional side window was fitted in lieu of the staircase panel. (Photograph: Tim Moore)

Delivered to Luton Corporation as 131–5 (XXE 131–5H) in December 1969, but not used, Eastern Counties acquired all five of these Bristol LHS and re-registered them with Norfolk marks as WNG 101–5H. These shorter LHs were easily identified by the small bay ahead of the emergency door. In 1977 the batch were renumbered LHS932–6 to make way for new Leyland Nationals. LHS934 (new as LHS937) is seen here on the occasional 545 service on 29 June 1979 on Castle Meadow, Norwich. (Photograph: Tim Moore)

This line-up of buses was captured on 5 March 1980 at Ipswich bus station and shows how the ECW top deck body style remained easily recognisable through several chassis types. Left to right we see: Bristol VRT/SL VR332 (NAG 587G); Bristol FLF6G FLF441 (GPW 441D); and Bristol FS5G X68 (50 CNG). VR332 had been new in July 1969 to Western SMT, while FLF441 had been new to Ipswich depot in January 1966, complete with a full rear destination display, which was later removed. X68 was new as LFS50 in June 1963, being converted into the Engineering Training Vehicle in August 1983 and was repainted into a blue/grey/yellow livery. (Photograph: Tim Moore)

1973, the year of the exchange of Lodekkas for Bristol VRs between the National Bus Company and the Scottish Bus Group, also saw some Lodekka exchanges locally, with Eastern Counties taking some from Lincolnshire Road Car and Eastern National. LWC 662C had been new to Eastern National in 1965, coming to neighbouring Eastern Counties in 1973 and gaining fleet number FLF426. She passed to Ben Jordan (dealer) of Coltishall in February 1980. (Photograph: Peter Horrex collection)

Eastern Counties received thirty Bristol VRTs from Scottish Bus Group companies in 1973 as part of the exchange of Bristol VRTs for Bristol FLFs with the National Bus Company. NGM 157G was a Bristol VRT/SL6G with an Eastern Coach Works seventy-seven seat body, new in 1969. She was numbered VR316 in the Eastern Counties fleet and is pictured in King's Lynn bus station on 31 July 1982. (Photograph: Robert Appleton)

One of the 1977 deliveries was LN583 (TVF 618R), a Leyland National 11351A/1R with standard fifty-two-seat bodywork, one of sixteen that year. It is seen at Central Works on 2 June 1977. All new LNs at that time were delivered with the last three digits of the production number shown in the destination box (in this case it was vehicle 04466), a practice which ceased a short time later. (Photograph: Tim Moore)

December 1981 was one of the severest winter months of the twentieth century. VR148 is seen heading towards Norwich city centre on North Walsham Road in Old Catton in that very cold month, though the weak winter sun would no doubt feel nice through the windscreen. Four star petrol at the time was priced at £1.65 a gallon, equivalent to around 37p a litre! (Photograph: Tim Moore)

After a break of five years, Eastern Counties took fifteen more Bristol LH saloons in 1977/8, this time with forty-three tan seats (plus luggage pen) and Leyland 0.401 engines delivering 138 bhp but retaining manual Turner Clark synchromesh transmission. LH928 (WEX 928S), a Bristol LH6L, is seen shortly after delivery outside Central Works in Cremorne Lane, Norwich, on 22 February 1978. (Photograph: Tim Moore)

In June 1983, LL800 (OEX 800W), a 1980 Leyland Leopard PSU3E/4R with Willowbrook bodywork, arrives at London Victoria on the 098 National Express service from Cambridge. The batch LL792–800 (OEX 792–800W) were a diverted order from East Kent. (Photograph: Tim Moore)

Eastern Counties took a total of 120 Bristol FS5G with sixty-seat Eastern Coach Works bodies between 1960 and 1965, numbered LFS1–55 and LFS62–126. Immaculate and straight from the paint shop in Cremorne Lane, LFS86 is seen here circumnavigating St Stephen's roundabout in Norwich, bound for Northfields on service 511 on 22 July 1980. Withdrawn in 1981, the bus was later renumbered X83 (not carried) and the company planned its conversion to a 'vintage replica'. However, the project never proceeded and the bus was sold to Cambus in January 1985, being exported to the Netherlands in 1993. (Photograph: Tim Moore)

Service vehicle X52 (NCL 549L) was a Ford Transit pickup truck, and is seen here at Silver Road in Norwich on 11 April 1980. For many years Fords were dominant in the service vehicle and staff car fleets. (Photograph: Tim Moore)

RLE875 (YAH 875J) was new in 1970, and was an RELL6G with ECW DP50F bodywork. A Saturday in January 1980 saw her loading passengers in Colchester while working for the East Bergholt outstation. (Photograph: Peter Horrex)

LL751 (MCL 933P) was a Leyland Leopard PSU3C/4R fitted with forty-nine coach seats in an Alexander T type body, new in 1976. LL751 was at March (Fountain) in April 1978, waiting to depart on service 344 to Peterborough. (Photograph: Robert Appleton)

On 29 May 1980, we see five Bristol FS resting in the evening sunshine at Norwich (Vulcan Road) after a hard day, having just been through the wash. Left to right we see: LFS79 (AVF 579B); LFS119 (FPW 319C); LFS86 (BNG 886B); LFS104 (DNG 404C); and LFS108 (DVF 108C). The buses date from 1964/5, and when seen they would have been fifteen years old but were still a good workhorse and just the right size to get through the traffic. (Photograph: Tim Moore)

VR412 (CJO 472R), a Bristol VRT/SL3 with Eastern Coach Works ultra-low-height bodywork, was new to City of Oxford Motor Services in 1977, and was one of three such vehicles purchased by Eastern Counties in August 1984 as VR410–2 (CJO 470–2R). The lack of a white band over the windscreen is an easy identifier of a very low height VR. (Photograph: Tim Moore)

Bristol FL6G LFL57 is seen on Castle Meadow, Norwich, on 15 March 1980, a year before withdrawal. Eastern Counties purchased six of these in the winter of 1962/3, numbered LFL56–61 (556–8 BNG and 559–61 BPW), all having Bristol engines and open platforms. LFL57 had platform doors fitted and was converted to Gardner 6LW power in 1972. It is now preserved. Note the offside illuminated advert panel, a trend in the early 1960s. (Photograph: Tim Moore)

This photo, taken in the Silver Road storage shed in Norwich in January 1980, shows newly delivered Leyland Leopards (carrying three different manufacturers bodywork) awaiting licencing. Unfortunately the only identifiable coach is LP814, nearest the camera. (Photograph: Tim Moore)

LL879 (XPW 879X) is seen here outside Central Works in Norwich after delivery from ECW on 22 July 1982. LL879 was one of fourteen Leyland Leopard PSU3G/4R chassis with ECW forty-seven-seat bodywork delivered in 1982. Following large deliveries of stage carriage buses in 1981 (Bristol VRTs and Leyland National 2s), 1982 and 1983 were notable for the company as it did not purchase any new buses, just coaches. (Photograph: Tim Moore)

VR301 (LFS 291F) was a Bristol VRTLL/6G new to Eastern Scottish and seated eighty-three passengers. This view, taken in Norwich on 3 July 1977, shows her about to depart for Cromer on service 763. (Photograph: Tim Moore)

This picture, taken in Surrey St depot in Norwich on Sunday 22 November 1981, shows a fine line-up of crew Lodekkas. Seen here left to right are: LFS91 (CNG 291B); FLF470 (KNG 470D); LFS101 (DNG 401C); and FLF447 (HPW 447D), plus six others. (Photograph: Tim Moore)

LL812 (JCL 812V) was a Leyland Leopard PSU3E/4R with forty-nine coach seats in a Willowbrook body, and was new in 1979. On 8 April 1980, LL812 was at Drummer Street bus station in Cambridge, working a journey on National Express service 098 from London (Victoria) to Norwich. (Photograph: Robert Appleton)

The beginning of the end for the Bristol REs with Eastern Counties based at Ipswich began in earnest in 1984. Here RL680 (RAH 680F) stands withdrawn at Ipswich in July of that year, having spent most, if not all, of her working life in East Suffolk. New in the summer of 1968, upon withdrawal she passed to Hartwood (exports) of Birdwell and was subsequently scrapped. (Photograph: Peter Horrex)

VR151 (JNG 49N) struggles through winter weather in Rose Lane, Norwich, in early 1987. This bus was one of ten Bristol VRT/SL2s with Eastern Coachworks bodywork added to the fleet in 1975, numbered VR151–60 (JNG 49–58N). (Photograph: Tim Moore)

Leyland Nationals were initially delivered with no colour relief, not even a white band, these being applied after delivery if required. By 1977 the Leyland roundel badge was not fitted at the factory, with the corporate image dictating the double-N symbol be placed between the headlamps. Seen here outside Central Works in Norwich is LN590 (WAH 590S) in October 1977; all preparatory work has been completed, though the delivery card is still in the nearside window! (Photograph: Tim Moore)

Dual-doored LM640/1 (KAH 640/1D) were delivered in December 1966, with mainly perimeter seating and standing for thirty passengers. Unsuccessful in service, they were returned to Eastern Coach Works in 1967 for conversion to standard forty-five-seat single-door configuration. The roof lights, which enabled standees to see out, were left in place after conversion and these buses were easily identified by this feature. LM641 is seen in Norwich on 29 June 1979. She was withdrawn shortly afterwards and became mobile office X77, finally going for scrap in August 1983. (Photograph: Tim Moore)

The location of this view is outside the Post Office Sorting Office on Thorpe Road, Norwich, where LFS 91 (CNG 291B) awaits its return journey to Bowthorpe (Wendene) on 12 June 1980. The bus was delivered in October 1964 and was withdrawn in May 1982, passing to APT at Bracebridge Heath. (Photograph: Tim Moore)

Minibus operation in Norwich commenced on the Cringleford and Eaton routes in October 1985 with Ford Transit vans converted by Carlyle. MB950–61 were eventually registered C950–61 YAH in lieu of the B prefixes reserved for them, though some arrived carrying B-TNG registrations, such as MB957, which is seen here in Norwich (Surrey Street) depot just after delivery. (Photograph: Tim Moore)

The morning sun reflects off Eastern Counties RL677 (PPW 677F) as she awaits her departure time at Shotley in 1981. New in 1968, she was withdrawn in 1982. (Photograph: Peter Horrex)

New in 1977, LL839 (SPW 105R) was a Leyland Leopard PSU3E/4R with forty-nine coach seats in a Plaxton Supreme body. She is pictured at Drummer Street bus station in Cambridge on 2 November 1981, working on service 797. Limited-stop services 797/798/799 linked Cambridge with London (Victoria), and they were jointly operated with London Country Bus Services (Green Line). (Photograph: Robert Appleton)

Seen in Norwich Central Works on 26 May 1978 is the second delivered Leyland National, LN540 (HVF 540L), which arrived just before Christmas 1972. In this view the bus is undergoing rear end accident repairs and clearly visible is the heating equipment mounted on the nearside roof, which is normally hidden under the pod. On the left of LN540 is a newly delivered VRTSL3, possibly one of the batch VR203–7. (Photograph: Tim Moore)

LN542 and LN543 (HVF 542/3L), seen here at Central Works on 15 February 1978, were delivered in February and March 1973 respectively, and were allocated to Norwich. Their type was 1151/1R/0401, and here they retain the stainless steel bumpers only fitted to very early models. On LN543, the small sticker showing the numeral 1 at the top centre of the windscreens relates to the destination blind variant fitted. (Photograph: Tim Moore)

Delivered in February 1962, LFS28 (2928 PW) was a Bristol FS5G with an Eastern Coach Works rear-entrance sixty-seat body. It is seen in this view at the top of Norwich bus station on 17 December 1977 shortly before withdrawal. In January 1978 it passed to Hartwood Exports at Barnsley, then Meynell of Carlton for scrap a few months later. Note the original offside illuminated advertisement panel fitted from new. (Photograph: Tim Moore)

RE848 (RPU 868M), seen at Ipswich in 1984, was one of a pair of 1974 Bristol RELH6Gs with Eastern Coach Works forty-seven-seat bodies purchased from National Travel (South East) in 1978, though they were originally ordered by Eastern National. The livery is the revised Eastline livery, applied in the by then standard venetian blind style. Seen here in summer 1984, the coach passed to Ambassador Travel on formation in September the same year. (Photograph: Peter Horrex)

New in November 1981 as a standard red seventy-four seater, VR285 (VEX 285X) was a Bristol VRT/SL3 with an Eastern Coach Works body. In early 1984, VRTs VR284–7 (VEX 284–7X) were sent back to Eastern Coach Works for conversion to sixty-six dual-purpose seats and a repaint to what had become known as the Redline livery. Seen after conversion operating a 790 to Cambridge, VR285 is at the top of Norwich bus station. The coach behind is a Crosville dual-purpose-liveried Bristol RELH with Eastern Coach Works bodywork, and is operating a National Express relief on service 952 to Manchester. (Photograph: Tim Moore)

RE851 (SAH 851M) was adorned in this livery and was supposed to be the regular vehicle used on the express Eastline 792 service between (initially) Ipswich and Cambridge, though this was later extended at each end to run between Felixstowe and Peterborough, and was operated jointly with Premier Travel. This view was taken at Ipswich in 1983. (Photograph: Peter Horrex)

Unfortunately, this view is undated, but it would probably have been taken in the mid-1980s. Three Bristol VRTs queue to attempt to climb up from Castle Meadow past the Bell Hotel in atrocious weather led by VR151 (JNG 49N). Shortly after this view was taken all buses were withdrawn and parked up due to the conditions. (Photograph: Tim Moore)

New in 1982, LL828 was a Leyland Leopard PSU3G/4R with forty-seven coach seats in her Eastern Coach Works body. Painted in British Rail livery to work the Peterborough–Wisbech–King's Lynn rail link service, LL828 was on layover outside Peterborough railway station on 31 December 1982 when seen. (Photograph: Robert Appleton)

Another view here of Eastern Counties RL677 (PPW 677F), this time passing through Lowestoft in September 1978. The earlier flat-screen examples of the Bristol RE (and indeed the LH) had shallow windscreens, causing problems for taller drivers. (Photograph: Peter Horrex)

Glasswells furniture store in Norwich commissioned an overall advertisement on Leyland National LN771 (XNG 771S) in January 1986, which is seen here at Castle Meadow in Norwich. The destination boxes of National Mark 1 buses suffered from a lot of dirt, both on the destination glass and blinds. The main cause of this was the heating 'pipes' feeding the demister, which passed through the destination boxes. (Photograph: Tim Moore)

One of twenty-two Bristol FS5Gs added to the fleet in 1965, LFS119 (FPW 319C) is at The Boundary in Norwich on 12 August 1980. The windscreen is open, indicating a warm day, though the screen tended to blow closed at higher speeds due to worn mechanisms! Heading in the opposite direction is an almost new Leyland National 2 operating a clockwise City Circle, the white band indicating this was one of the first deliveries, numbered LN601–4. (Photograph: Tim Moore)

New in the spring of 1973, Eastern Counties LN549 (HVF 549L) is seen here at Wickham Market in 1983, working the first Saturday morning journey of the day from Stradbroke to Ipswich in the care of the Woodbridge outstation. By now the outstation at Stradbroke was a one-man, weekday-only operation. (Photograph: Peter Horrex)

In 1981, consideration was being given to the re-bodying of Bristol RELH/ECW RE894–8 (SVF 894–8G) with new ECW B51 bodywork, and body removal and chassis reconditioning had commenced when the project was abruptly abandoned in favour of new Leyland Leopards. The first batch of three B51s were numbered LL826–8 (WEX 826–8X) and were delivered in March 1982. LL828 is seen before delivery at ECW in Lowestoft on 25 February 1982. The attractive red and blue stripes were changed to grey bands from the next batch, and the white headlamp surrounds seen here were changed to black before delivery. (Photograph: Tim Moore)

New in December 1970, Eastern Counties RL739 (AAH 739J) survived in the fleet until 1986, when she was withdrawn and sold via Wigley of Carlton to Holladay (Red Bus Services). In 1988 she moved to Hoare of Chickerell (Bluebird Coaches) and then in 1996 to Vintage Yellow Buses, kept at Poole, before being broken up for spares by March 2002. This view was taken at Shotley in 1980. (Photograph: Peter Horrex)

Back in March 1983 we see LH930 (WEX 930S) in Surrey St bus station, Norwich. Delivered as a standard forty-three-seat bus in 1978, she was repainted into this special Commuter Express livery for the Holt commuter service in February 1983, at the same time being down-seated to thirty-nine using coach seats from withdrawn Eastern Coach Works-bodied Bristol RELHs. (Photograph: Tim Moore)

LFS118 (FAH 118C) was a Bristol FS5G Lodekka with an Eastern Coach Works sixty-seat body, new in 1965. On 8 April 1980, LFS118 was at Cambridge railway station, working the cross-city service 181 through Cambridge city centre to Kings Hedges Road on the north side of Cambridge. (Photograph: Robert Appleton)

In August 1985, Leyland National LN763 (XNG 763S) was repainted into this overall advert on a white base for Norwich BMW dealer Averills. LN763 was new in April 1978 and is seen here in Surrey Street depot before entering service in its new colours. White is never a good choice for a base colour and the choice of white wheels was a bad one. (Photograph: Tim Moore)

A pair of flat-screened Bristol VRs stand in Ipswich in 1980. Eastern Counties' own VR396 (ENG 396K) stands under cover, while ex-Scottish Bus Group's LFS 281F awaits her next journey. (Photograph: Peter Horrex)

Brand-new Ford Transits with Dormobile converted bodies stand in Norwich bus station after delivery and before the blinds were fitted. The Dormobiles were superior to the first batch (which carried Carlyle bodies) and were numbered MB962–84 (C962–84 YAH). All were delivered in September 1985. (Photograph: Tim Moore)

LH910 (YAH 910J), a Bristol LH6P new in 1970, is being prepared for repainting at Central Works, having had several panels replaced, including the fibreglass front valance. A brand-new VRT/SL3 stands alongside. (Photograph: Tim Moore)

Seen at Ipswich in 1984 is Bristol RELL RL737 (AAH 737J), having been withdrawn. It stands alongside driver training bus Bristol Lodekka 97TVX, which had been new to neighbouring Eastern National in 1960. She was purchased in 1978 (see page 50) by Eastern Counties for the purpose of being converted to a driver training bus, and she survived in the fleet until 1987. (Photograph: Peter Horrex)

The original vehicle used for publicity work in Norwich was ex-Ribble Leyland Leopard LL836 (HRN 951G), renumbered X81 in the service vehicle fleet from September 1982. In 1983 the company acquired a dual-door Bristol LH from Hants & Dorset (REL 743H) for publicity use and numbered this X82 to replace X81. The vehicle is shown at Norwich (Bell Avenue) on the traditional stands used for coach bookings and excursions during 1984. (Photograph: Tim Moore)

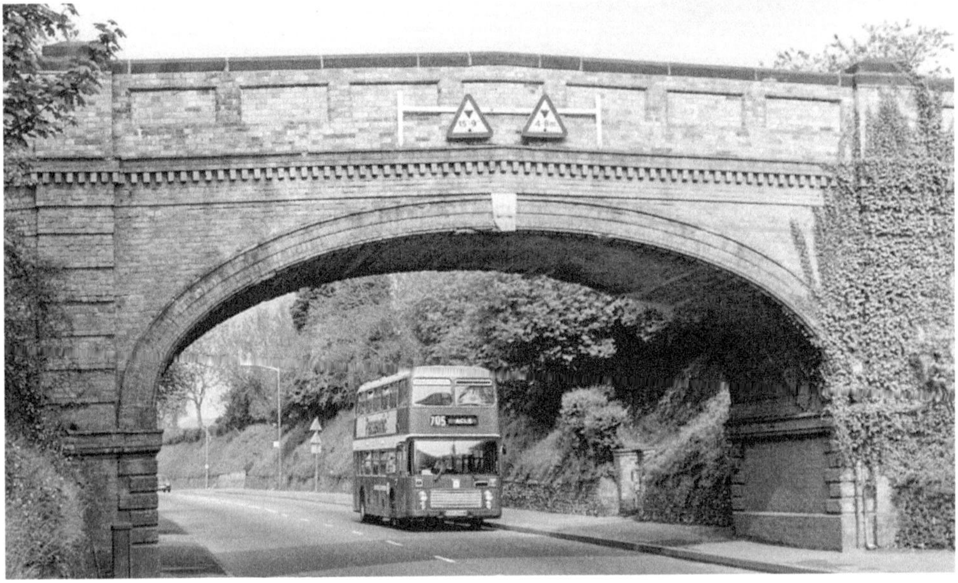

Probably the most famous bus in the Eastern Counties fleet, VR266 (RAH 266W), a VRTSL3, was new in 1981. Seen here passing under the bridge outside St Andrew's Hospital in Norwich, she is en route to Acle via Brundall and Blofield. In 1988 she was to suffer an incident that made world headlines when she was partially swallowed by a hole in Norwich after an old chalk working collapsed. The damage was quite minor, however, and several more years of service followed. (Photograph: Tim Moore)

Transferred from Lincolnshire Road Car Company to Eastern Counties in 1973 as part of the National Bus Company/Scottish Bus Group Bristol FLF/VRT exchanges, VFE 959 was a Bristol FLF6G Lodekka with an Eastern Coach Works seventy-seat body, and was new in 1963. Given fleet number FLF431, on 2 November 1981 she was in St Andrews Street in Cambridge, working cross-city service 185 from North Arbury to the New Hospital (Addenbrooke's). (Photograph: Robert Appleton)

RL520 (HPW 520L), photographed in November 1972, is seen in Norwich bus station only a few days after entering service, having arrived from Cromer. It had arrived in standard Tilling red livery with a cream band even after some buses had been repainted into NBC poppy red, and the decision was made to merely apply a wide white band to cover the cream band and black beading together with NBC fleetnames and grey wheels. Given some buses were carrying an experimental dark red and white NBC livery, they did not look too bad. (Photograph: Tim Moore)

In 1962 the standard new coach for Eastern Counties was the Bristol MW6G with a Gardner 6HLW engine and Eastern Coach Works thirty-nine-seat bodywork, though a few had thirty-two reclining seats for tours. LS807 (3807 PW) was one of twenty delivered that year, and in this view LS807 has been repainted in the original white National coach livery with small underlined fleetnames over the front wheels. The location is Harford Cattle Market in Norwich during the Driver of the Year heats on 19 August 1973. (Photograph: Tim Moore)

Seen at Castle Meadow, Norwich, on 14 August 1980 is VR224 (BVG 224T), which is sporting an advertisement for Barratt Homes. New in October 1978, this Bristol VRT/SL3 had standard seventy-four-seat bodywork by Eastern Coach Works. This wrap-around type of advertisement was officially called a 'Unibus' style, with all-over adverts being termed 'Colourbus', and this particular advert was carried by many UK buses at the time. (Photograph: Tim Moore)

RL507 (CNG 507K) was a standard Eastern Coach Works-bodied Bristol RELL that was delivered new in September 1971. In this view she is seen in Bury St Edmunds in August 1982, with less than two years left to go before being scrapped in the summer of 1984. (Photograph: Peter Horrex collection)

The last of the eight Norfolk Flyer-liveried Leyland Tigers, LT894 (EAH 894Y) was selected for exhibition at the twenty-ninth Brighton Coach Rally, and is seen here in glorious sunshine on Madeira Drive on Brighton's seafront on 24 April 1983. (Photograph: Tim Moore)

In 1977, Eastern Counties selected two-year-old VR144 (GNG 710N) as its Queen's Silver Jubilee bus, and sponsorship was provided by Queensway Warehouse in Norwich, a furniture and carpet retailer, on whose premises EC had parked vehicles in the 1970s as an overflow to the Surrey Street depot. This view of VR144, fresh from its repaint, was taken at Britannia Barracks on St James' Hill in Norwich in December 1976. (Photograph: Tim Moore)

RL690 (YJB 523H) was acquired from Alder Valley in 1981, and is photographed here inside Ely depot during August 1982. She passed to Edmunds of Rassau sometime in 1986, and was scrapped by 1989, having been burnt out in a fire while in service in 1987. (Photograph: Peter Horrex collection)

RL683 (RAH 683F) was a Bristol RELL6G with an Eastern Coach Works fifty-three seat body, new in 1968. On 4 July 1981, RL683 was in Peterborough city centre, working cross-city service 384 from Bretton to Westwood. She was crew-operated, and is seen with the conductor about to help lift an intending passenger's shopping trolley aboard. (Photograph: Robert Appleton)

Since 1975 Eastern Counties had worked in partnership with Norfolk County Council in the provision of community buses. MB991–3 (A991–3 LVG) were 1984 Ford Transits with Mellor bodywork seating sixteen passengers, and MB991/3 are seen in Surrey Street, Norwich, awaiting use. These were for Sharrington and Docking respectively, with the third (MB992) being destined for Aldborough. (Photograph: Tim Moore)

Passing through the leafy lanes of Suffolk back in 1981, Eastern Counties RL668 (PPW 668F) heads out of Newbourne, bound for Waldringfield on service 241. (Photograph: Peter Horrex)

In 1978, Eastern Counties acquired four Bristol RELH6G with Plaxton forty-seven-seat bodies (RE844–7, LWC 979–82J) from National Travel (South East) Ltd. By the time this picture was taken of RE846 in June 1983 in the shadow of Thaxted's fifteenth-century Guildhall, the coach had been updated with comfortable re-trimmed seats from withdrawn ECW-bodied RELHs. (Photograph: Tim Moore)

There are some quite photogenic locations across East Anglia featuring historic buildings, and one of the nicest is Wymondham Cross. VR218 (BVG 218T), a standard seventy-four-seat Bristol VRT/SL3 with ECW bodywork delivered in October 1978, is seen here at the historic Wymondham Cross, heading to Norwich on a glorious day in the summer of 1984. (Photograph: Tim Moore)

RLE746 (GCL 348N) is seen here at Felixstowe during 1981. One of a batch of eight Bristol RELH6L delivered in 1974 with Leyland 0.680 engines, the ECW bus shell bodywork carried forty-nine dual-purpose seats. The whole batch was converted to Gardner 6HLX power after a few years in service. (Photograph: Peter Horrex)

VR260 (RAH 260W), with seventy-four bus seats, is loading in Norwich bus station in August 1984 as a National Express 747 relief to Cambridge. The 'Jockey' all-over Colourbus advert had been applied in February that year, and the vehicle was to be transferred to the newly formed Cambus Ltd fleet the following month. (Photograph: Tim Moore)

One of the benefits of driving the LFS class was the ability to open the windscreen on hot days, provided you accepted a little dust and fumes from other traffic! On a hot 22 July 1980, LFS101 (DNG 401C) swings into St Stephen's Street from Westlegate in Norwich. This Bristol FS5G was new in January 1965 and passed to Mike Flynn for preservation in February 1983 before being exported to Poland in 1991. (Photograph: Tim Moore)

FLF468 (KAH 468D) was a Bristol FLF6G Lodekka with an Eastern Coach Works seventy-seat body, new in 1966. Sixteen years later, on 13 April 1982, FLF468 was still hard at work, and is pictured in Queensgate bus station in Peterborough while working on cross-city service 384 from Bretton to Westwood. This was the last year of Bristol FLF and crew operation at Peterborough, which mainly finished on 31 December 1982. On 1 January 1983, Peterborough city services were revised and renumbered. (Photograph: Robert Appleton)

RL667 (PPW 667F) stands withdrawn at Ipswich in 1984 at a time withdrawals of Bristol REs was gaining pace. RE848 (RPU 868M) stands to the right. (Photograph: Peter Horrex)

New in 1980, LN619 (PEX 619W) was a Leyland National 2 with a Leyland engine and forty-nine seats, and was 11.6 metres long. It is pictured at Drummer Street bus station in Cambridge on 4 July 1981. (Photograph: Robert Appleton)

A few changeovers still existed into the 1980s. In this view, taken in 1984, LN563 (PVF 363R) has arrived at Swaffham Market Place from King's Lynn, while out of shot VR372 has arrived from Norwich. The Norwich driver will now cross the road and take LN563 onwards to Norwich while the VR would continue to King's Lynn with the driver who brought out the National. (Photograph: Tim Moore)

RL516 (EPW 516K) arrives at Peterborough in June 1984. New in April 1972, she passed to Cambus upon the split of Eastern Counties, and then passed to a number of other operators before entering preservation in 2005. She has changed hands a couple of times since then, but still survives today in Norfolk and is regularly seen out and about. (Photograph: Peter Horrex collection)

LH703 was the Bristol LH prototype with chassis designation LHX6P. The forty-five-seat body (number EX12) was by Eastern Coach Works and the bus was new in February 1968 as a demonstrator with Bristol Commercial Vehicles, passing to Eastern Counties in January 1970 as LH719. When new it had the unloved shallow windscreen but was modified in the early 1970s. In February 1977 it was renumbered to LH703, and is seen in Norwich on 28 May 1977. (Photograph: Peter Horrex collection)

In the years before privatisation, Central Works in Norwich provided new and reconditioned parts and supplies to all the depots across the company's area. X47 (PVG 816J) was a Ford D600 lorry used for the collection and delivery of such parts and is seen here at Cremorne Lane in February 1976. New in 1971 and delivered in maroon, it had received NBC poppy red the previous year. (Photograph: Tim Moore)

To assist with the transition to all one-man operation in early 1984, three Bristol VRT/SL6Gs were hired from Eastern National (SMS 40/4H, and OCS 576H). The latter is seen here in January 1984 during its five-month stay, during which time it retained EN livery with the obligatory 'On Hire' stickers, being known as T47 by the company but not carrying this number. (Photograph: Tim Moore)

A busy scene at Drummer Street bus station in Cambridge on 26 February 1983. VR391 (DAH 391K) will travel north to Ely and King's Lynn on service 409, while VR387 (BNG 448J) will travel south to Royston on service 146. Both were Bristol VRT series 2s new in 1971. In the background Bristol VRT series 3 VR161 (MCL 937P), new in 1976, has arrived on service 151 from Peterborough. (Photograph: Robert Appleton)

VR377 (UAH 377G) stands at Stonham Aspal in Suffolk on a wet day in 1979 before working local service 240 back into Stowmarket. Delivered new in June 1969, she was an early withdrawal in the summer of 1981, and was subsequently scrapped. (Photograph: Peter Horrex)

It is a tradition at the Derby for open-top buses to provide spectators with a good view of the race while enjoying on-board hospitality provided by specialist caterers. In 1986 all five Eastern Counties open-toppers were hired for the Derby and spent the night in London before the big day. Seen here in Battersea on the morning of the race, 4 June 1986, are OT3 (JNG 50N), which was new as VR152, and OT4 (NCK 980J), which was acquired from Ribble the previous year and intended to be VR380 but which was converted to open-top instead. (Photograph: Tim Moore)

Probably numerically the last coach purchased before Ambassador Travel was split from Eastern Counties, ML905 (A668 XDA) was one of three Metroliners acquired from Midland Red (Express) Ltd, arriving on 15 August 1984. Despite carrying Ambassador Travel fleetnames, ML903–5 (A666–8 XDA) were owned by Eastern Counties before being transferred to the new Ambassador Travel (Norwich) Ltd in September that year. (Photograph: Tim Moore)

In the early years of Cambridge Park and Ride services, VR408 (HAL 104K) was seen collecting passengers in Emmanuel Street, Cambridge, on 10 March 1984. VR408 was a Bristol VRT/SL6G with an Eastern Coach Works seventy-seat body, new to East Midland in 1971, and acquired by Eastern Counties in 1983. (Photograph: Robert Appleton)

RL727 (YPW 727J) is photographed in Lowestoft in August 1982. Delivered new to the company in the summer of 1970, she was withdrawn in 1983 and sold to Bailey of Biddisham, and then to Hoare of Chickerell in 1992, before being scrapped in June 1994. (Photograph: Peter Horrex)

The winter of 1986 saw several days of snow, and buses struggled with the conditions. Seen in Norwich, St Stephen's Street, is one of the Dormobile-bodied Ford Transits recently introduced onto the Cringleford and Eaton services, unidentifiable due to the accumulation of snow. On the opposite side of the road is one of the four high-bridge VRs (HVR 331–4) bought from Hastings & District, recognisable by the yellow band and roof. (Photograph: Tim Moore)

Pictured in Needham Market in Suffolk in 1979 is Eastern Counties VR368 (TNG 368G). Delivered new in May 1969, her exact date of withdrawal is not known, but she was noted on site at Ipswich during the winter of 1985 into 1986, being stripped for spares. (Photograph: Peter Horrex)

RL674 (PPW 674F) was one of twenty Bristol RELL6Gs with Eastern Coach Works fifty-three-seat bodywork new in 1968 with the shallow windscreen, which was a feature of early flat-front RELLs. RL674 is seen here on Ipswich Road in Norwich en route to Locksley Road terminus of service 552 in the spring of 1985. She was withdrawn the following year and sold for scrap. (Photograph: Tim Moore)

On 9 September 1974, Eastern Counties was split up, with the western area bus services transferred to a new company Cambus. New in 1974, VR131 (RAH 131M) was a series 2 Bristol VRT/SL6G with an Eastern Coach Works seventy-four-seat body. On 28 September 1974, VR131 was seen in Queensgate bus station at Peterborough, still in National Bus Company poppy red livery, but with Cambus fleetnames. Later, VR131 was renumbered 620 in the Cambus fleet. (Photograph: Robert Appleton)

Seen outside Central Works on 23 February 1978 before entering service at Norwich, VR205 was one of five buses with XNG registrations delivered that month (VR203–7). Three months later she was to become much less anonymous when selected to be repainted as the 'Anywhere bus', receiving an all-over advertisement for the company's all-day tickets, which she carried for several years. (Photograph: Tim Moore)

X59 (49 CNG) had been new in May 1963. A Bristol FS5G, she was one of many Lodekkas across the United Kingdom that saw extended lives working as a towing vehicle. Eastern Counties converted her in February 1975, and she continued in this role until withdrawal some fourteen years later, in 1989. (Photograph: Peter Horrex collection)

VR285 (VEX 285X) was a Bristol VRT/SL3/6LXB with an Eastern Coach Works seventy-four-seat body, new in 1981. In 1984 she returned to Eastern Coach Works to be fitted with sixty-six semi-coach seats, and received a repaint into Redline livery. Allocated to King's Lynn, on 5 June 1985 VR285 was pictured in Queensgate bus station at Peterborough while working limited-stop Eastline service 794 to King's Lynn and Norwich, the predecessor to today's First Excel service. (Photograph: Robert Appleton)

The last official day of crew operation in Norwich was 31 December 1983, and in this view FLF452 (JAH 552D), a 1966 Bristol FLF6G with seventy-seat ECW bodywork, is awaiting its last departure to Costessey on Castle Meadow. (Photograph: Tim Moore)

Following the Transits of 1985, some larger twenty-seat Mercedes L608Ds were ordered for 1986.Delivered in February 1986, MA713 (C713 BEX) has Alexander converted bodywork, hence the MA designation. It is seen here (before fleet numbers or the destination blind were added) in Surrey Street depot during a break in training duties. (Photograph: Tim Moore)

MD997 (NAH 142P), which was a Ford A0609 with Alexander twenty-five-seat dual-purpose bodywork, was purchased as part of a trial batch within NBC. Delivered in all-over cream on 15 April 1976, it had received NBC dual-purpose livery by the time this photograph was taken outside Central Works in Norwich on 30 April 1976. Obviously unsuccessful, it was withdrawn after three years' service. (Photograph: Tim Moore)

VR185 (PEX 385R), seen on 10 August 1982 in Hunstanton bus station, was a standard VRT/SL3 with an ECW seventy-four-seat body. A National Holidays-liveried VRT on an excursion stands behind, probably VR298 or VR299. (Photograph: Tim Moore)

# Biography (Peter Horrex)

Peter Horrex grew up in Kesgrave on the outskirts of Ipswich in Suffolk during the 1960s and 1970s, becoming interested in buses in 1976 after his first ride on a Bristol Lodekka. In 1986 he made the decision to move to London to work as a bus driver, passing through London Transport's Chiswick training school later that same year. He has driven many types of bus in service, both in London and Ipswich, and currently drives buses for Arriva in London.

# Biography (Tim Moore)

Born in Norwich, Tim Moore joined Eastern Counties in 1975, working at Head Office in Norwich for three years before a short period at Crosville Motor Services. He returned to Norwich in 1979, re-joining Eastern Counties, and worked the following twenty-five years driving at all the Norwich depots before moving to a training role in 2004. In 2006 he moved to Konectbus as Training Manager, and now works at Lynx in King's Lynn.

# References


PSV Circle newssheets

PSV Circle Eastern Counties fleet history (publication)

http://bcv.robsly.com/index.html

http://www.buslistsontheweb.co.uk/